I AM MY OWN CHOCOLATE

New & Renewed Poems

by

Cedric Brown

I Am My Own Chocolate

© 2025 by Cedric Brown

ISBN: 978-0-9857006-8-3

Junie's Mood Press

None of this work was generated
by Artificial Intelligence

PREFACE

I just might be a creature of habit. Twenty years ago I photocopied and distributed a chapbook of poems, *The Path to Here,* to family, friends, and colleagues. Ten years ago I published *Tar Heel Born*, the narrative poem series reflecting on a hot-and-cold relationship with my home state. Five years ago, during the first months of the pandemic, I wrote and published an ebook of very short "starter stories," *You Are Everything*.

After a five year hibernation, the Junie's Mood muse again tapped me on the shoulder, which has resulted in this collection of poems, new and renewed. Only a few of these pieces have seen the gaze of eyes other than my own, so I'm happy to get these out into the world.

The photo interludes are meant to provide a palate cleanse, perhaps setting a mood for what's to come. These are photos from my phone camera, all capturing poetic moments both meaningful and mundane snapped during the course of a regular day.

Lastly, I was surprised to read in an old journal that my high school self once told a substitute teacher "I am my own chocolate." I love that teenaged playfulness and racialized cheek. I hope I have never lost that spirit of self-discovery and joy. We all should be our own chocolate. Or whatever brings you delight, which is critical to hold onto amidst the troubles of these times.

Cedric Brown
Winston-Salem, NC USA
September 2025

Why I Am an Introvert

behind closed doors i don't have to be perfect
have to know every answer to every question
every number & fact
which syllable is stressed & accented
eveready with quick quips or snap clapbacks
competently confident, confidently competent

don't have to be wrinkle & pimple-free
pecs pressed, shoes screaming coolness
cap signifying, tat warning

behind the door
tongue can be tied
logic faulty, rethought
private cracks aired out
inside jokes made aplenty

naked mind running free
just hangin out
with my own
self

2022

I AM MY OWN CHOCOLATE

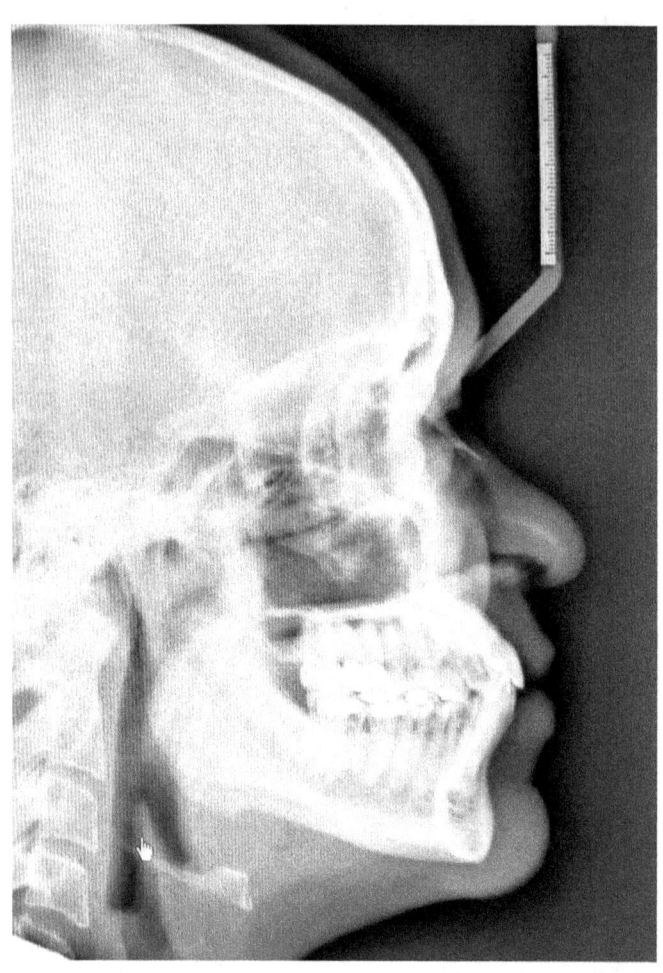

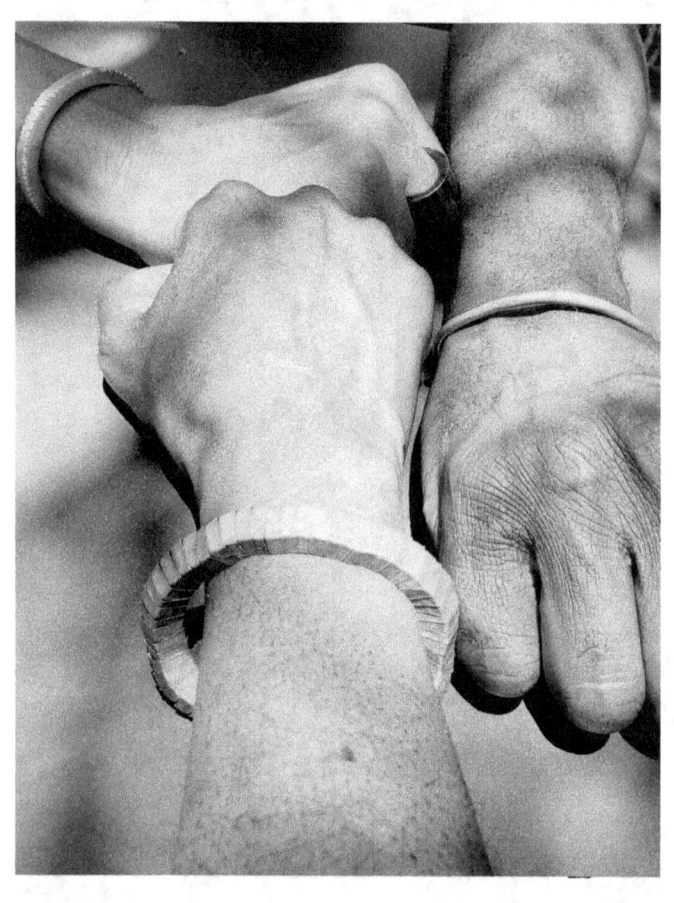

Giraffe Esteem

once i gave up on becoming a panther
sleek + muscular, prowling
close to the ground

+ grew to embrace my own knobby knees + slender neck,
stilts as legs

i began to see elegance in
my own movement,
see the beauty from treetops

2024

Ode to Cakes

he had them
bounce somethin hard off em
kinda cakes
them kunta kinte runnin the hundred
kinda cakes
them "why is my mouth waterin"
kinda cakes
them "u may be a top but i wanna hit that"
kinda cakes
them "if those are your cakes what else u packin?"
kinda cakes
them "i turnt u out & didnt even touch u"
kinda cakes
them "even cakes wanna rub them cakes"
kinda cakes
them "if i knew u were comin i'd a baked a cake"
kinda
cakes

2020

yo love

is a warm lavender bath
i immerse myself
& later emerge
humming a secret melody

1987

Untitled Haiku

wax candle drippings
like lovers seed on my chest
they cool just the same

1990

Divorcee Haiku

too many assume
that afterwards you're broken
rather than breathing

2025

F Grammar

i still crave the magic of that thing
sure the fullness of pleasure & pain but
moreover the validation of my own appeal
of my own visibility

we cannot bring forth new life
but u can renew my own
if just for the moment
that's how deep it is
how deep it needs to be

since there is no fucking without
u & i

2025

Third Time Charm

in the first chapter
Love
was the realm of grownups
mushy soap opera romances that made me squirm
watching white men & women kiss
over & over

or it was pious & required:
for Jesus
& family
in that order
though i may have co-opted the term
for birthday cake & christmas toys

otherwise it was a vague feeling now & then
for people whose presence made me happy,
a yearning laying in wait

chapter II
at 13 i started to chase the feeling
that had crystallized into a magnetic draw to certain boys
who made my toes curl when they
strutted into the classroom
whose names i'd scribble on notebook paper
then tear into tiny pieces, paranoid

that feeling went unspoken
& for years, went unrecognized, unreturned, unvalued
leaving me to wonder
what was so wrong with me
that i couldn't catch this contagious thing

& when it was finally returned to me
as a thirtysomething
it was still tinged with disappointment:
elation with expectation
sweet but on occasion sour
comforting but confining

sometimes middling, sometimes muddling
sometimes performative

in Chapter III
with more years behind than ahead
i hope i've learned the lessons from the first eras: that
Love is all of these things, expansive
a higher state of being
beyond the craving & crash

welcomed when
nourishing but not addictive
joyous but not manic

now leaving me
contented
with life's delights
like a lingering sweet
aftertaste

2025

BEAUTY IS EVERY DAY

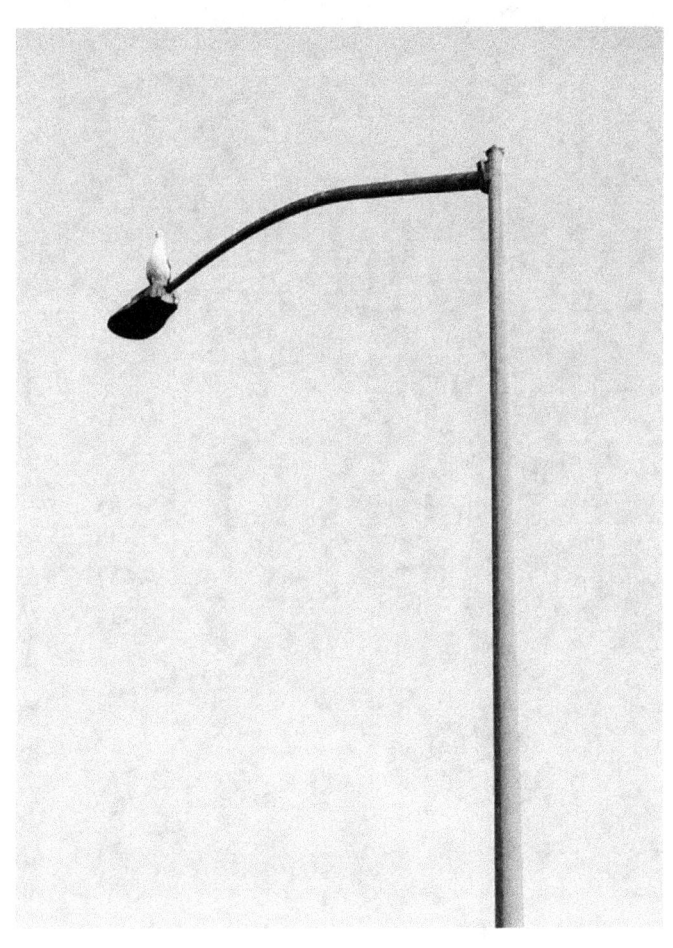

Sakura

u would not believe these cherry blossoms
branches popping with bright floral hope
sprinkling over grass like pink pastel snow
confetti celebrating the onset of spring
like yayyyyy we did it
welcome back

2020

Neighbors

This sheltering slowdown & our thicket-facing back deck allow for splendid bird watching

We're fortunate to live in their neighborhood,
Waking up to insistent chirps/song & witnessing their busy business the whole day through

Inhaling heavily-perfumed humidity,
we blow good luck kisses to swooping bright cardinals, our reincarnated family reassuring us
in these trying times

We note nesting robins & staccato-necked sparrows
tall athletic bluejays & black speckled woodpeckers
groundhopping wren & sultry-throated mockingbirds

We crane in wonder to see
soaring high high
an ominous wide-winged bird of prey
(I couldn't tell what)
riding the low sky currents

Wild they remain,
not as our entertainment but a graceful reminder
to our bumbling selves
that we too are in an ecosystem
bigger than the latest videoconference

& we say thank you
avians,
Amen

2020

second chance for blackberries

blackberries remind me of my grandmother's
hot summertime cobblers,
dark purple juice bubbling over sweet biscuity crust

i didn't like blackberries at first
(though i loved my grandma)
their tiny seeds the same crunchy nothing
as ants
which, yes, i once ate live from the ground

later in life
i didn't like blackberri either
that dreadlocked black queer blues singer

thought he also was a crunchy nothing
after the one time he cussed me out on the phone

time passed & we became friends
& laughed about it

sadly i didn't know his govt name
until he was gone

now, like then
blackberries get a second chance
i appreciate that plump dark fruit
casting springtime lightness on my palate

2024

reminder to self

are u in love with what u got
not more atop more atop more / atop
capitalist culture driving u to believe
your life is meaningless / without reprieve

are u in love with what u have created
a masterpiece life that u have curated
not an empty shell of accumulated things
but a thoughtful collection of substance that sings

are u in love with what u got
are u a bit happy every day, full stop
can u recognize what it means to be blessed
and recall lessons from the times of big stress

over job or lovers or money or fame
or envisioning dreams that never quite came
but your body is working / your income is stable
a roof's over head and food's on the table

you've a gracious plenty / what more do u need
when does longing for more start to look like greed
not necessities that help you grow and evolve
but with needless acquiring, maintain your resolve

to not compare yourself to your neighbor the Joneses
to run the rat race / play the dos and don'tses
that curtail your spirit from being happy and free
that keep you from living authentically

in the midst of challenge / be still and re-center
remember that spring always follows the winter
stay grounded in the good that you hold to be true
and know what makes up the best of u

are u in love with what u got
not more atop more atop more / atop
maybe just maybe your life is just right

divinely aligned / God is holding us tight
so let's continue to fight the good fight
and on that note i will bid you good night

2022

BETTER IS A NEXT STEP

Old Man

No matter how old I get
I'll never be comfortable with
The N Word
Will likely never get free from
the sharp jab to the gut
or the crisp slap to the face
when i hear it uttered:
-er
-a
-uh
In any form
but particularly from people
who should know better

Maybe the memory of being on
the receiving end is too fresh
Spat in my 10 year old face from trash lips
Or being ever painfully aware of its ugly origins,
the violence implied in its threat:
The horror of the Klan memorabilia
on display at the main library downtown
Or a flyer in Mineral Springs of "the coming race war"

The NAACP tried to bury it in 2007
held a sanctified funeral and everything
But true to its white supremacist DNA
It came roaring back strong as ever

Maybe I could work it out if we left it
in the realm of a slur, an expletive
Exclusively to express hatred and disdain
such that letting it loose would be a point of no return,
like muthaFUCKAH
ain't no going back

Coopting and reclaiming and
casually slanging it about with a begrudging affection
just dont work for me

As Omotosho said
In our infinite creativity as a people,
We couldn't think of nothing
BETTER?
No more colorful, incisive way
to express ourselves
given our mastery of new trends and colloquialisms?

N is the chitlins of the English language
no matter how u dress up those whitefolk leftovers
that shit still stink

2025

How to Be a Good Black Guest in an African Nation*
(A Briefing for Us Bougies)

*With respect, gratitude, and apologies to Binyavanga Wainaina

Know where you're going, place-wise.
Learn people's names and pronounce them correctly. Or attempt to. If you can pronounce all those Biblical names, you can pronounce these African ones. Use that phonics training.

Learn at least two phrases in a local, non-colonizer language. Slang in French, Portuguese, English, Dutch, German--and some might add Arabic and Chinese--don't count either.

Don't complain about food.
Don't complain about electricity.
Don't complain about insects or other animals, except life-threatening ones. Complain about snakes at any time and all times.
Speaking of which, don't complain about timeliness.
And for once, don't complain.

Understand some of the national history.

Be aware of income inequality and power differentials.
Flatter where possible without being patronizing.
Or just be polite at all times.

Ask a peer from that nation what is and isn't culturally acceptable.

Know that some folks embrace the idea of diaspora, and others will look at you like a dangerous or crazy stranger. Resist the urge to expect a welcome home message from everyone. They might just be trying to figure you out.

Also resist the urge to gape open-mouthed at Africans—Black ones—on the money, the adverts, the newscast, at the mall, and everywhere imaginable. It is, after all, their continent.

These are real Africans, so don't try to out-African them. Slow down with the fabrics and trinkets.

You might feel like a totally brainwashed Westerner in their presence. Most of us are and have been. It's not all you; it's mostly a much larger system at work.

But that's okay, you're trying. At least you're here.

And who says families
are all alike
anyway.

2022

Crossfire

it's disappointing to have to declare aloud that

all people deserve to live in peace and safety
within their historic homelands and beyond

and that

genocide is never, ever acceptable

disappointing since

one side is unclear on these concepts
despite the evidence

and

the other side is uncertain about where your loyalties lie
despite the evidence

2025

Dear Gigi,

Please forgive us for the many
days turned into years
whizzing around in cars
complaining about gas prices & oil changes & insurance claims
Find enough love in your heart to forgive us
jet setting the globe in destination wanderlust
Keen on business class luxuries as we got older
Please forgive us for the novelty of
wood-burning fireplaces & the ease
of single-use paper products
holding our addiction to beef

It didn't used to rain like this
And certainly wasn't this hot all the time
Really, we didn't used to wear masks in every season
(At least not 'til the month and year you were born)
Or ask Siri to think for us

Really, we used to be fun and smart
And sit around on the front porch at your great-
grandparents' house
singing and telling stories
and making up games to play
and reading the latest from the children's library
and acting out scenarios from TV

Besides
I'll be able to tell if you
spit on my grave
I won't be surprised
but still
you might as well forgive us
now

2022

Hardly

if so-called illegals were gonna take over
they would've already done it
poisoning food in fields & restaurants
booby-trapping plumbing & appliances
disappearing kids from daycare
tucking razors into hospital-cornered beds
all i know is
when i talk to students without documents
about their dreams & aspirations
i hear human stories
community stories
american dream stories
that aren't diluted because they
love soccer or sopes or sinaloa
the threat to this nation
is from within:
pledging allegiance to whiteness
and the gaslighting for which it stands
will never render complete
our brilliant promise

2006

All I'll Say: a Haiku

Let's remember why
Woke was coined in the first place:
To stay vigilant

2025

Grounding (for Panta Rhea)

remember that in daylight
our star the sun
obscures millions of others like it
that sprinkle the night sky
holding us in awe of their distance & beauty
u are part of this picture
u are but one part of this picture

remember your feet are now planted on ground
that thousands of others have trod over eternities
so while u may be trailblazing
it's not upon virgin terrain

remember that it took 500 ancestors
over an octet of generations,
even more even further back
facing untold hardship in their now namelessness
all leading to u
in this place today

so in that spirit
stop
breathe in the abundance
the abundance that surrounds u constantly
sit awestruck
in the vastness of the universe
plant your feet
on well-trod ground
celebrate being
the impossible dreams of your forebearers

open your eyes
& live
forward

2024

YOUR HEART BEATS A SONG

Where I'm Coming From
(From "I Swing Like That" Performance Piece)

What is this sound
This singing stinging soothing smoothing
sometimes sexing sometimes vexing sound called
America's indigenous music
Black folk's classical
Our gift to the world
Birthed at the mouth of the Mississippi, N'Awlins
Delivered by the big names
Billie & Bix & Benny
Dizzy & Dinah & Duke
With Miles to go & Tranes to ride
Goin' to hear Art with Ella's fellas
The muscles of Armstrong & the serenity of a Monk
The voices of generations
Charlestons & Harlem renaissances
Chi-town, the Big Easy, Kansas City

Jazz was/they were
telling stories of everyday people

We were living on Bon Air Avenue
just the five of us kids and lil Mommy

i knew i was different 'cause
i really didn't care about grandmaster flash or
the sugar hill gang or kurtis blow
couldn't rap "the message" if you paid me
i was excited by donny hathaway IN PERFORMANCE
playing NU-PO at Carnegie hall
my sista won the album offa the radio

Mommy shoulda known
when she played "swingin' shepard's blues"
over and over at my request
til i could sing it myself

& they laughed
when i had the nerve to turn the stereo to instrumentals
while we ate spam in mustard sauce for dinner
& they laughed
when i usedta sing
in half-lit room in front of the mirror
& they laughed
when i listened closely
to intercom elevator music

then they got mad
when i dreamt of something better than what i was,
where i was
wearing old denim from goodwill
& sharing a room with two footballer brothers

jazz, you promised intimate little clubs tucked into an urban blocks
where blue illuminates the stage
except for a single spotlight
that falls on a stool at the center

you promised men in suits & women sitting with long crossed-legs
chattering about the cool things city people chat about
& sipping on drinks out of sleek glassware

you hinted at intelligence & dignity
without rigidity of whitebreadedness
of good times
without dark & hot drunkenness
of other places & adventures
& languages & style
they couldn't
& wouldn't
promise me in suburban north cackylacky

i wanted to be in your tribe

didn't want to be in the band
i wanted to sing
didn't want to read the music
i wanted to sing
didn't want to sit
i wanted to sing!

still telling the stories of
everyday people

2003

If I Lived Inside Donny Hathaway's Voice

I would always be warm
whether wearing an open necked daishiki,
kaleidoscopic pattern embroidered on the chest
Or ribbed turtleneck,
Shielded against the cold white winter
ever blowing outside

My 4C would be perfectly Afro shaped and sheened,
glistening like so many stars a-twinkle
in the vast blackness of the universe

My pad would be right-sized, comfy
adorned with tasteful midcentury modern decor
Orange as a feature color
Shona sculpture standing sentinel straight,
my guardian angel

I would be forever warm and forever safe
Thankful as church reverence
Soulful as pinto beans spooned from a bowl
Complex as 800 languages in the Diaspora merging into
One people

Inside Donny Hathaway's voice

2022

Too-Hep Cat
(From "I Swing Like That" Performance Piece)

what about a man like Dizzy
'cause he was fun to be around, ya know?
the whole beret and goatee and bebop glasses and
how he thrust his hips on the downbeat
ooo i wished that horn was me, twisted into new shapes
having that hot John Birks breath blowing thru
alla my holes
mmph, what about Dizzy
can he be like Dizzy?

whaddya think of Miles Davis?
i mean, before he started beatin on people
young and black and brooding
loved that sleekness
that cool
the skin that shines like oil
so dark you see the colors of the rainbow
trumpet standing straight at attention
gleaming and hard
can he look like a young Miles?

then again, there's Max Roach!
Max Roach just did it for me!
that bangin and poundin and pattin and tappin
he was gonna be my revolutionary jazz hero
on toms, snare, and cymbals
my black superman with a square jawline,
kickin ass and takin names
and i'd scream out an aria for Freedom Now
while he bangs and pounds and pats and taps some more
a man who can handle his sticks
hittin that taut skin in just the right way
where is my Max Roach?

2003

Blues in Twos

i.
the blues ain't nothin but God
or did u forget that among
the blinding blondness of angels

the blues aint nothin but a trick
to get u to calm yourself from
skippin thru life on blissful cherry sidewalks

is nature's way of slowin your fast-self down
so u can consider the scenery

in the end
the blues ain't nothin
(but the power u give em)

ii.
Not in a blue space
Blues aint gonna catch me
Not in a blues place
Blue just let me be

I got tales to tell
Feasts to fix
When done with that
Might find an new trick

Got lightnin to cast
Got storms to churn
Got mountains to leap
Got cash to burn

Got a village to raise
Plenty crops to reap
And after all that
Gonna get some sleep

Too much to do
To be down with blues
U a pretty color, true
But ain't got time for u

2003

Shoe Devil Blues

Well I just met the devil
He was a fine honey-colored man
I just met the devil
He was a fine honey-colored man
Well, he poked me with his pitchfork
And put back on his wedding band

Well I met him at the shoe store
Trying on a pair of shoes
I never ever thought
I'd be buying a case of the blues

I invited him into my living room
He glided into my bed
I got him outta my house
But I can't get him outta my head

I just met the devil
He was a fine hunk of a man
Welllll he poked me with his pitchfork
And put back on his wedding band

1999

Sometimes These Things Happen

I won't cry
when we say goodbye
'Cause the love not the tears
is everlasting

I won't regret
Though my heart has yet
to release the thrill I felt
when with you

So now we go our separate ways
Sometimes these things happen
Both in search of better days
Sometimes these things happen
And although we couldn't be
I only wish you godspeed
With a kiss set upon the breeze

I won't pine
because time after time
I'll still smile
when I recall certain memories

No, I won't mourn
Nor look back with new scorn
The song says love and set
the loved one free

Although we tried to make it right
Sometimes these things happen
Resist the urge to flee or fight
Sometimes these things happen
And no we cannot be just friends
Or say we'll ever meet again
Because we all must say goodbye
Because we all must say goodbye

1998

DO REMEMBER ME
(JE ME SOUVIENS)

Home for Randall

Randall was always a country boy
Even all that time in New York
Didn't rid him of Chinquapin in 'im

Skin like rich dark soil
Jowls like full of pork & greens
Voice husky like smokehouse mist
Countenance like prayer
Words like deep King James version
Wisdom like grandfather minister

Creating magic from nothing
Our Marquez (like Terri McMillan said)
He left us too soon but we always know
Through the legacy of his words

We
can
go back
home

2021

Red, for Ella Ruth Archie

Red demands to be remembered not because it is demanding but
because its presence never lets us forget

Red threatens to shake you to pieces yet
you understand where that fierceness comes from,
soundly anchored in a scarlet pulsing heart
Red wraps you in breathtaking hugs & ensures
that you are welcomed
Is a tiny celebration each day

Red is cherry Kool-Aid & strawberry shortcake sweet
Is mother wit curling off the tongue, honey

Red has solitary moments like
the cardinal song pitched from high in the pines
or a petunia stretching sunward
by the corner of the house

Red, a diva decked in a sharp-brimmed Sunday hat,
is prepared to receive the Good Word.
Red encourages us to live in courage & truth,
understanding that the price paid for our freedom
is crimson

Red is to be cherished & held ceramic tenderly
though it itself is brick solid

Red demands to be remembered because
it's impossible to forget something as
fundamental as your own blood
racing rubies through your every capillary

Red shows up devoutly, daily
so we regularly recall what it's like
to be unquestionably
Loved.

2017

Like Sisters
For Camille from Cookie

Sometimes the space between
friend & sister
is as thin as a candy wrapper
or popsicle stick
or notebook paper
& in the early years,
the difference between
sister & friend
is barely distinguishable
even though you don't have the same parents
or live under the same roof
even though you
love your blood sisters but
need your space
to figure out your own self

She's the one you tell your quiet thoughts
about who's cute & who thinks they cute
about little slights & big dreams
& sometimes
about your struggles
or advice on hers

She's the one you sit out on the steps with until the
street lights start to buzz & you know it's time to
get home but there's just this one other little thing
to share

She's the one that
you can't remember how she arrived in your life
but she was just always there
laughing & calling your nickname

As single days deepen into years
the two of you grow & experience similar milestones,
perhaps miles away
but not apart

The thin line between friend & sister
becomes measured by gift wrap & greeting cards
& maybe letters & tissue
Through marriages & babies & birthdays,
Kids' graduations & relationship changes,
aging parents & transitions
But your reunions by phone & certainly in person
snap you back into place
like you were sitting on the steps again
sharing (with) an unwavering trust and adoration
girly giggles now hearty grown hahas

She's just there
laughing & calling your name
until the grey day when present
becomes past
& you say to others
"She was my friend
who was like a sister to me"
holding her dear in your heart
always

2021

Letter to Paula

"Partire è un po' morire."
leaving is like dying
a little

your departure marks
my miniscule death
a void unfilled

by denial
false hope
tears

i miss you already

1986

regrouping

did i forget jazz
did i forget dee dee bridgewater & abbey lincoln
that "music is the magic of a seeeecret world"
always within
did i forget another country & paris & joe trace & harlem
did i forget romare bearden & william h. johnson
canvas & acrylics
cutouts & collages & the contemplative excitement of the gallery space
did i forget dance
old skool, house & yes, vintage 80s madonna
getting into the groove lucky star borderline burnin up
did i forget celia & salsa &
humid nights under havana stars
brazilian bahia beats & ass quivering sambas
did i forget poetry
free verse & headlands & the good feeling of reading
loud & long & black & strong
nikki & langston
did i forget the hot glare of spotlights & cool chills
from appreciative applause
did i forget myself as an artist
i think i almost did
i think i almost
did i think
i almost
forgot
me

2015

Being a Poet

What's special about being a poet
Can anybody do it
The label feels heavy, grand
Pressure to be deep, opaque
outre even, to be called brilliant
Taken seriously by literati who
take themselves seriously

What's special about being a poet
Walking around thinking about
life in stanzas & metaphors
the mashup of reflection & language
the economical use & strategic placement of words,
perfect for an introvert

What is special about being a poet is
Always being connected to your own thoughts
(At times, too much so)
& the movements of others
Relishing opportunities to be a bit eccentric
saying odd things pointedly
pointed things oddly

But the specialest thing
to me
Is the magic of turning
ordinary moments into
gems worth considering,
an every day type of
alchemy

2025

THE END

MANY THANKS

Creative Crew: Aliona, Charles, Derek, Joe, Rebekah

Cheerleading Squad: Andrea, Andreana, Catherine Claire, Ellen & Bryan, Larry, Patrick, Reggie, Retha, Sharnita, Tony

Eagle eyes: Odysseus, Stewart, Wambūi

And of course my family, the Archie Brown Douglas Alans

ENDNOTES

Because I miss liner notes on albums

Yo Love: Although referring to an unrequited desire, this is still one of my favorite-ever poems, written as a tender 19 year old.

Untitled Haiku: A version of this was published in Assoto Saint's *The Road Before Us: 100 Black Gay Poets* under Cedric Levon, back when I was nervous about using my full government name on a sex poem. This version is slightly different than that published one.

Second Chance for Blackberries: blackberri (1945-2021), the dreadlocked black gay Blues musician, was a tremendous cultural force in queer communities over five decades. His songs *Beautiful Black Man* and the haunting *Blues for Langston* were showpieces of the landmark 1989 Isaac Julien film *Looking for Langston*. blackberri was also known for his HIV advocacy and activism as well as his practice as a Lucumi priest.

Old Man, Note 1: An exhibit of Klan materials was opened for display at the Forsyth County (NC) Central Library on February 26, 1978, causing a clash between American Nazi sympathizers and Black protestors, who shut down the exhibition in two hours. As a 6th grader, I saw this on the news as well as overheard my grandparents expressing great insult that such a display was even considered, regardless of the First Amendment.

Old Man, Note 2: Omotosho is the Nigerian name bestowed on Dr. Daniel Black—professor, scholar, and author of *Black on Black* and several novels focusing on Black gay men as central characters.

Good Black Guest: Fashioned after Binyavanga Wainaina's funny but scorching satirical essay, *How To Write About Africa,* challenging often-repeated stereotypes and clichés.

Dear Gigi,: Named for my youngest niece but dedicated to all nine of my nieces and nephews.

Hardly: Back when I worked with undergraduates, several of the students in my program were undocumented. They were among the most talented and most driven of the bunch. This piece was no doubt written with them in mind, part of a personal education about immigration policy.

Grounding: It amazed me to consider, when I did the back-of-napkin math, how many pairs of ancestors it took to lead to a single present-day individual.

Where I'm Coming From: This and *Too Hep Cat* are excerpts from my 2003 performance *I Swing Like That*, a commentary on queerness in jazz, staged as part of an artist-in-residency at San Francisco's Jon Sims Center for the Arts.

Blues in Twos: To be clear, the blues are low grade and temporary. Depression is real. Seek help.

Shoe Devil Blues and *Sometimes These Things Happen:* Back when I sang with bands and music groups, I occasionally wrote songs, some of them based on true stories.

Do Remember Me (Je Me Souviens): This isn't a translation; it's a call-and-response between subject and writer. (Not that I think in French.)

Home for Randall: Randall Kenan (1963-2020)

Red, for Ella Ruth Archie: My beloved grandmother (1922-2017)

Like Sisters: For my mom's best friend, who was like another aunt to me

ABOUT THE AUTHOR

CEDRIC BROWN is an author of mostly short form nonfiction and poetry. His work is also included in *Blacktino Queer Performance, Outwrite DC, Africa Is a Country,* and *The Road Before Us: 100 Black Gay Poets*. Cedric is the founder of the Jacobs/Jones African American Literary Prize, sponsored by the North Carolina Writers Network, and co-founder of the Randall Kenan Prize for Black LGBTQ Fiction, sponsored by Lambda Literary. He lives in Winston-Salem, North Carolina, USA.

ALSO BY CEDRIC BROWN AND JUNIE'S MOOD PRESS:

Eyes of Water & Stone:
From Havana with Love

Tar Heel Born: A Native Son Speaks on
Race, Religion, & Reconciliation

You Are Everything:
10 Starter Stories

Tastes Like Chicken:
Travel Tales & Tidbits

All titles available through Bookshop.org

PO Box 17506
Winston-Salem, NC 27116
juniesmoodpress.com

None of this work was generated by
Artificial Intelligence.

All photos by Cedric Brown, taken in Winston-Salem, NC
except where noted

<u>I Am My Own Chocolate</u>

p.3	2020
p.4	2022
p.5	Key West, FL. 2024
p.6	2024
p.7	Nags Head, NC. 2025

<u>Beauty Is Every Day</u>

p.17	Lisbon, Portugal. 2025
p.18	2025
p.19	Lansing, NC. 2023
p.20	Emeryville, CA. 2020
p.21	2020
p.22	Highlands, NC. 2019
p.23	San Francisco, CA. 2025

<u>Better Is A Next Step</u>

p.31	Lisbon, Portugal. 2025
p.32	Oakland, CA. 2025
p.33	2021
p.34	2020
p.35	2020
p.36	Newark, NJ. 2024

<u>Your Heart Beats a Song</u>

p.47	Tarrytown, NY. 2025
p.48	East Bend, NC. 2025
p.49	Paretz, Germany. 2024
p.50	Dublin, Ireland. 2023
p.51	Oaxaca, Mexico. 2023
p.52	Ermioni-Hydra, Greece. 2023
p.53	Tampa, FL. 2021
p.54	2020

Do Remember Me (Je Me Souviens)
p.65	Palm Springs, CA. 2025
p.66	2025
p.67	St. Lawrence Gap, Barbados. 2025
p.68	Flushing Meadows, NY. 2023
p.69	2022
p.70	2019

Closing
p.77	2018

www.ingramcontent.com/pod-product-compliance
Lightning Source LLC
Chambersburg PA
CBHW051956290426
44110CB00015B/2260